T0389955

SAVE OUR EARTH!
Climate Action Explained

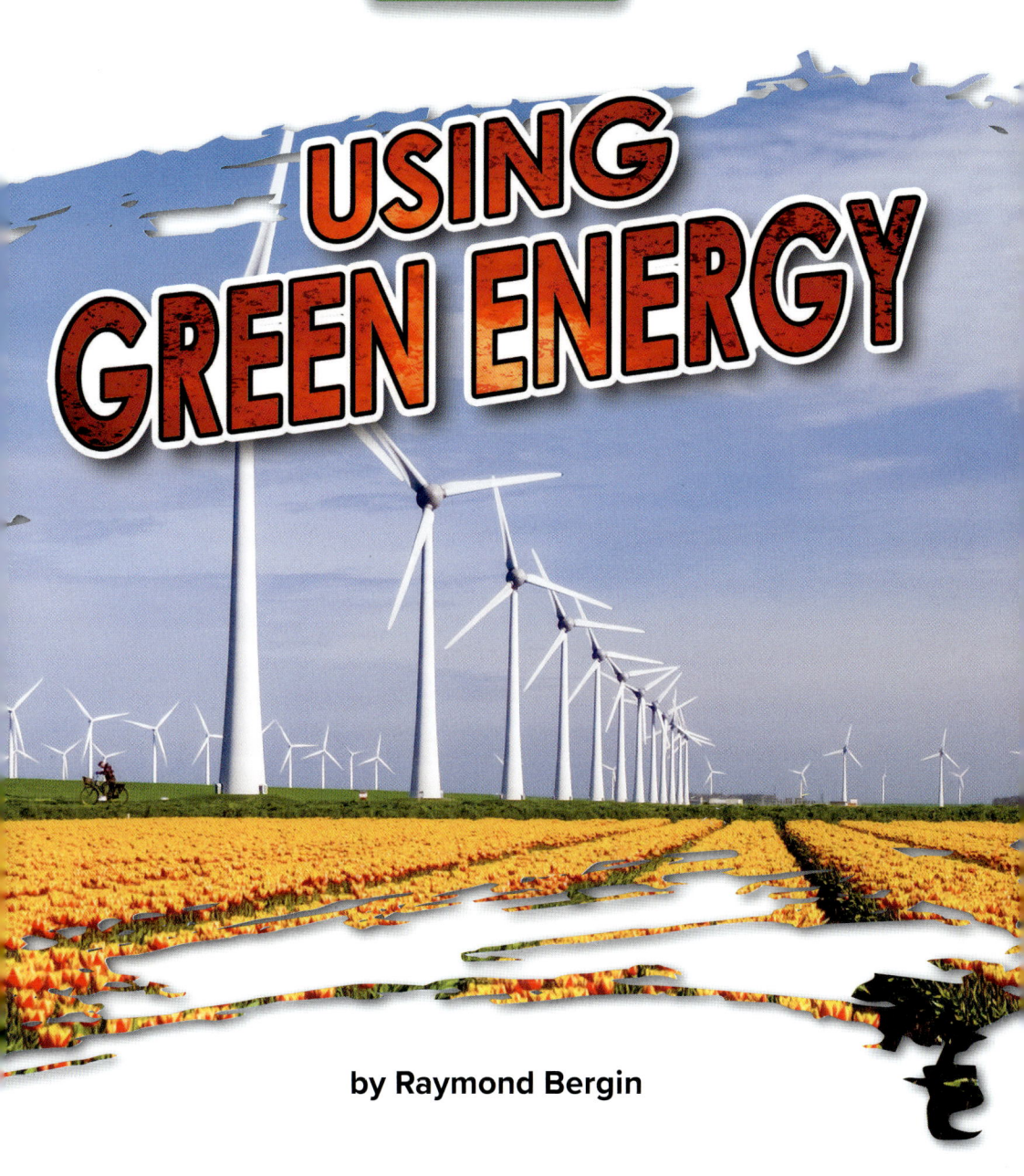

USING GREEN ENERGY

by Raymond Bergin

BEARPORT
PUBLISHING

Minneapolis, Minnesota

Credits

Cover and title page, © fokke baarssen/Shutterstock; 4–5, © Fahroni/Shutterstock; 6–7, © BlueRingMedia/Shutterstock; 8–9, © Susan Vineyard/Adobe Stock; 10–11, © travelview/iStock; 13TL, © Andrew Mayovskyy/Adobe Stock; 13TR, © Andy Dean Photography/Adobe Stock; 13BL, © rob245/Adobe Stock; 13BR, © Jacek Nowak/Alamy Stock Photo; 14–15, © vectorpocket/Adobe Stock and © KKT Madhusanka/Adobe Stock; 16–17, © inga spence/Alamy Stock Photo; 18–19, © Ian Forsyth/Getty Images; 21, © PA Images/Alamy Stock Photo; 23, © Bryan Bedder/Getty Images; 23BR, © onurdongel/iStock; 25, © Kamil Krzaczynski/Getty Images; 26, © Chris Van Lennep/Adobe Stock; 26–27, © Rungroj pakdeejoho/Shutterstock; 28, © Kunlathida/Adobe Stock; 29TL, © Greenseas/iStock; 29UML, © Andrey Popov/Adobe Stock; 29ML, © Isabel Eve/Shutterstock; 29BML, © Oriol Roca fotografia/Shutterstock; 29BL, © Mongkolchon Akesin/iStock

Bearport Publishing Company Product Development Team

Publisher: Jen Jenson; Director of Product Development: Spencer Brinker; Managing Editor: Allison Juda; Editor: Cole Nelson; Associate Editor: Tiana Tran; Production Editor: Naomi Reich; Designer: Kim Jones; Designer: Kayla Eggert; Designer: Steve Scheluchin; Production Specialist: Owen Hamlin

Statement on Usage of Generative Artificial Intelligence

Bearport Publishing remains committed to publishing high-quality nonfiction books. Therefore, we restrict the use of generative AI to ensure accuracy of all text and visual components pertaining to a book's subject. See BearportPublishing.com for details.

Library of Congress Cataloging-in-Publication Data is available at www.loc.gov or upon request from the publisher.

ISBN: 979-8-89577-050-4 (hardcover)
ISBN: 979-8-89577-167-9 (ebook)

Contents

A New Kind of Energy 4

Energy to Burn 6

Running Out of Fuel 8

Pollution with Power 10

Clean and Green 12

Harvesting Sunlight: Midong PV Farm 14

In Hot Water: The Geysers 16

Catch the Wind: Dogger Bank Wind Farm . . . 18

Battery Boost: Reeddi Portable Energy 20

Help from Hydrogen: Electrolyser 22

Catch and Clean: LanzaTech 24

Renewing Our Future 26

Go Green! 28

Glossary 30

Read More 31

Learn More Online 31

Index 32

About the Author 32

A New Kind of Energy

Exhaust pours out from cars heading toward the gas station to fill up their tanks. Not far away, a factory burns through **fossil fuels** nonstop to keep the assembly line running. Just outside of the hazy city, however, the scene is very different. Energy is coming from the world around us. Black solar panels glint in the sunlight. A network of pipes carries steam from deep underground. And huge wind **turbines** spin in the distance. What on Earth is going on with energy?

People around the world are switching energy sources. If current trends continue, solar power—energy taken from the sun—may be the world's number one power source by 2050.

Energy to Burn

Our modern world requires a lot of energy. Most cars, businesses, and homes get their power from fossil fuels. These fuels take a long time to form. They come from the remains of ancient plants and animals that were buried under layers of **sediment** millions of years ago. Over time, they were put under intense heat and pressure. This caused the plant and animal matter to turn into coal, oil, and natural gas. When burned, fossil fuels release energy.

Some fossil fuels are processed into other forms. Gasoline comes from oil. Natural gas can be turned into propane, which is used to heat homes and cook food.

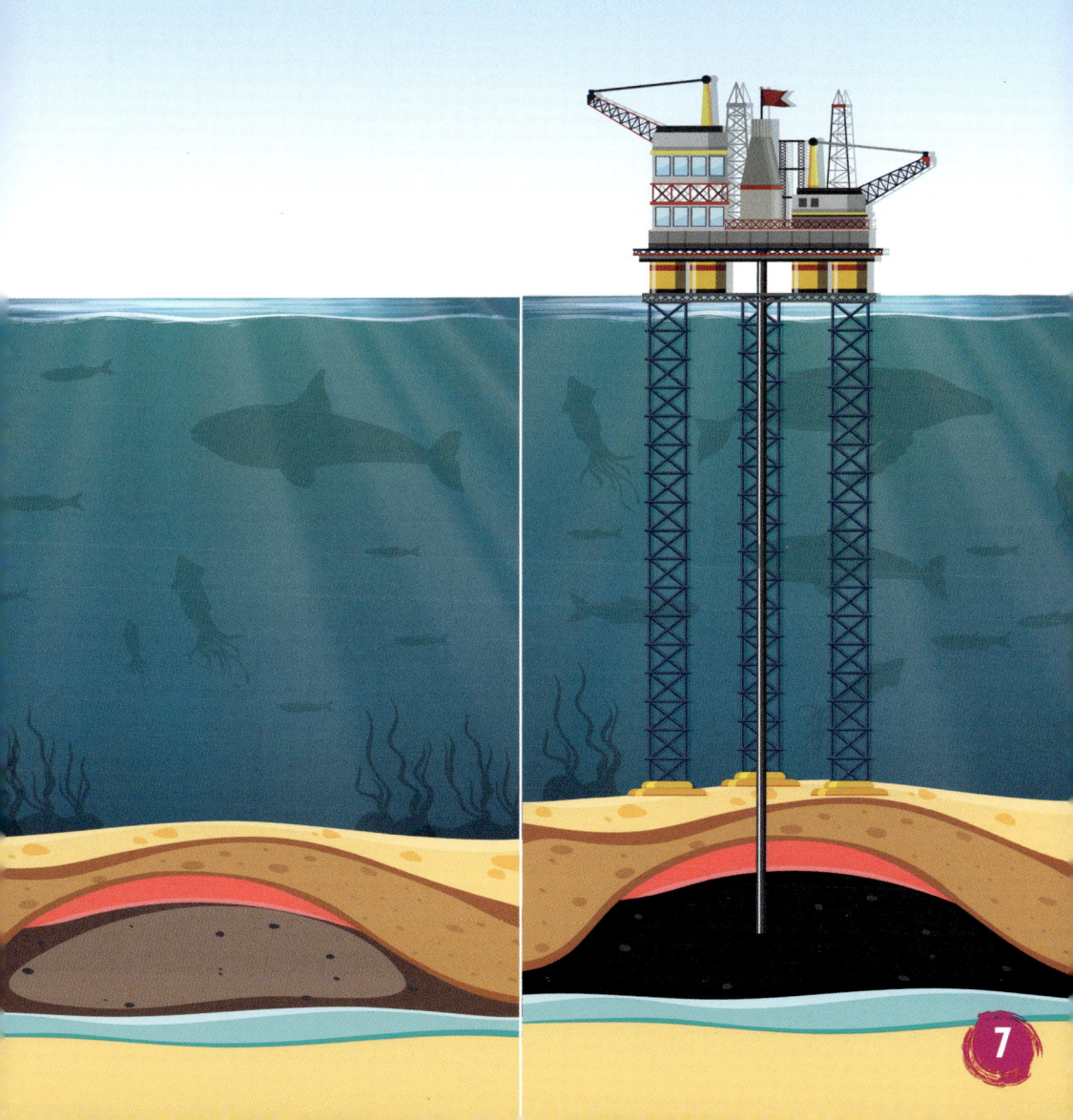

Running Out of Fuel

There are currently more than eight billion people on Earth, and experts predict there will be an additional two billion by 2050. As the population grows, so does our demand for energy. While burning fossil fuels currently provides most of the electricity, heat, and power we need, they won't last forever. Once they are used, fossil fuels are gone, and they cannot be replaced quickly. We are burning these fuels far faster than the millions of years it takes for them to form. If we continue to use them at our current rate, there may be none left in a century.

It is estimated that oil will run out by 2052. Natural gas may dry up by 2060, and coal could disappear by 2090.

Fossil fuels are brought to Earth's surface by drilling, mining, and fracking.

Pollution with Power

Using fossil fuels also comes at a heavy cost to life on Earth. When fossil fuels are burned, they spew harmful gases into the **atmosphere**. This pollution can result in allergies, heart attacks, asthma, and lung cancer. Fossil fuel pollution is blamed for about 20 percent of deaths worldwide.

Some of these gases also heat up our planet. Similar to how the glass walls of a greenhouse keep the building warm inside, these so-called **greenhouse gases** trap heat around Earth. This is making air and water temperatures rise.

Global warming is impacting many habitats. Warmer water is killing life in the oceans, and melting ice is transforming polar habitats. Hotter weather is drying up wetlands and rainforests.

Burning fossil fuels also releases chemicals and tiny, harmful particles into the air.

11

Clean and Green

To keep our planet powered while also staying cool and healthy, we must stop relying on fossil fuels. Luckily, there are several energy alternatives that are gentler on the planet. These are collectively known as green energy.

Green energy **harnesses** the forces of nature. We've learned to use sunlight, the movement of wind and water, and underground heat to create power. This energy can be collected, stored, and used without the harmful effects that come from burning fossil fuels. Green energy is also a **renewable** resource. There is a continuous supply of it.

Many green energy systems use turbines. Moving air, water, and steam sets the blades of the turbines spinning. This creates the energy that can be used to generate electricity.

Almost 30 percent of the world's electricity now comes from renewable energy sources.

13

Harvesting Sunlight
Midong PV Farm

Sunlight is the ultimate renewable resource. People worldwide use solar panels to collect and harness the sun's energy. **Photovoltaic** (PV) cells in the panels absorb sunlight and turn its energy into a current of electricity.

Light from the sun is made of tiny particles called photons.

Photons travel to solar panels.

Photons knock electrons free from atoms within the panels' solar cells.

Moving electrons create an electric current. They pass through layers of the solar cells.

The world's largest collection of solar panels, known as a solar farm, can be found in the desert landscape of Urumqi, China. The Midong PV farm has more than 5 million solar panels spread across an area the size of New York City.

China has also built the world's largest offshore solar farm. This farm features almost 3,000 PV platforms on the water, each the size of two basketball courts.

The current flows from the panel. Then, it is converted and used or stored for later use.

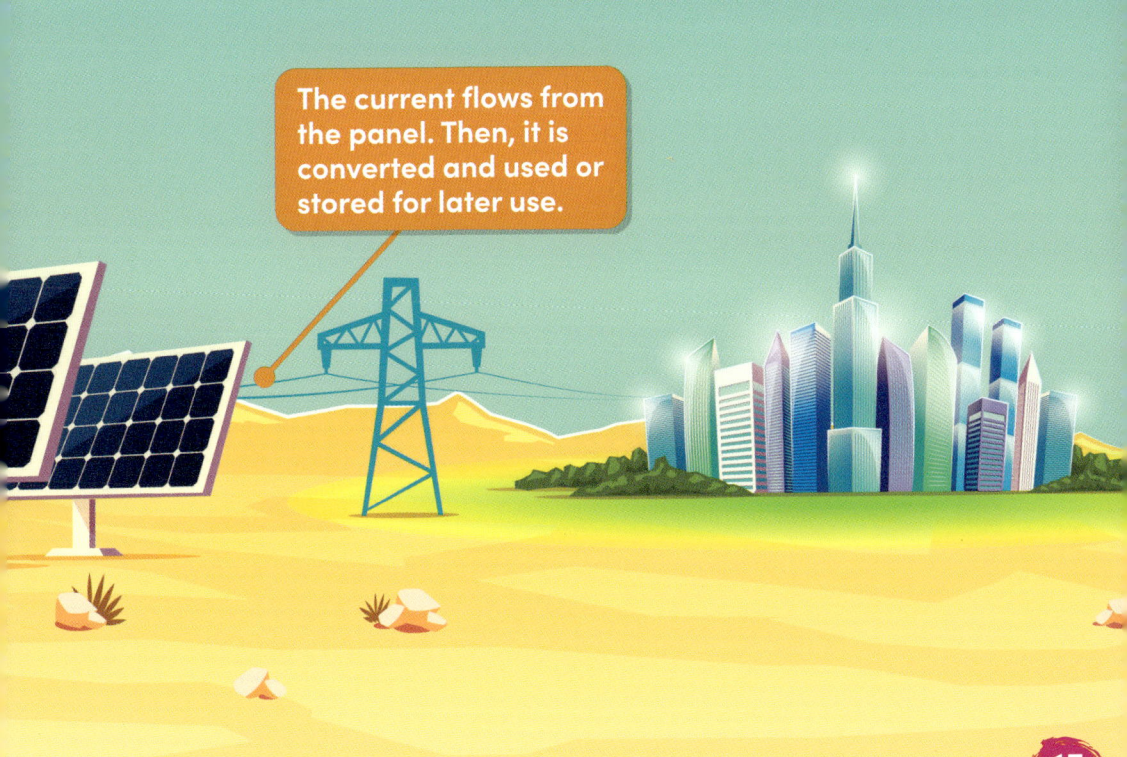

In Hot Water
The Geysers

Deep underground, Earth's superheated core turns nearby **reservoirs** of water into steam. This steam can then be used as a source of green energy known as **geothermal** energy.

The Geysers, located north of San Francisco, California, is the world's largest geothermal complex. It includes a collection of 13 power plants that pump up steam from Earth's heated underground reservoirs. This steam is used to spin turbines that generate electricity. In total, the complex gathers enough geothermal energy to power a city the size of San Francisco.

To keep geothermal energy renewable, underground water needs to be replaced. So, the Geysers pump wastewater back down to the reservoirs. They replace about 20 million gallons (76 million L) of water every day.

17

Catch the Wind
Dogger Bank Wind Farm

Humans have harnessed the renewable power of wind for centuries. Ships have long sailed in the breeze, and the first windmill dates to about 500 CE.

Each turbine blade on this wind farm is 117 yards (107 m) long.

Today, many modern wind turbines are clustered in groups called farms. They are often built at sea because winds above the ocean are stronger and steadier. The Dogger Bank Wind Farm in the North Sea is more than twice the size of any previous offshore farm. Its 277 turbines are able to power more than 6 million homes.

The longer a wind turbine's blades, the more electricity it can make. Just one rotation of a single turbine's blades on the Dogger Bank Wind Farm creates enough electricity to power a home for two days.

Battery Boost
Reeddi Portable Energy

Most large green energy projects are built to supply power to entire cities and regions. But a company called Reeddi has developed small-scale, inexpensive green energy options. Ordinary individuals can use these products at home.

Reeddi makes portable solar-powered batteries called energy capsules. These batteries can provide electricity to televisions, laptops, and lights. Reeddi's larger energy boxes can power most of a home's devices and appliances—even when they are being used at the same time.

Reeddi's energy capsules can be rented from vending-machine-like stations. They cost only 50 cents a day and have a 4-year lifespan. A single charge of a capsule lasts about 24 hours.

Olugbenga Olubanjo, founder and CEO of Reeddi, came up with the idea for the portable energy company while he was in college.

Help from Hydrogen
Electrolyser

The sun is such an immense energy source because it is made of the power-packed gas **hydrogen**. However, harnessing the energy of this gas is difficult. Most methods of **isolating** hydrogen on Earth release greenhouse gases in the process.

However, a company called Enapter has found a cleaner way. It turns water—which is made of hydrogen and **oxygen**—into green hydrogen. Enapter's Electrolyser device sends electrical currents through water to break apart its hydrogen and oxygen **molecules**. The device then captures and stores the separated hydrogen to be used as a clean-burning fuel.

Electrolyser devices come in different sizes. They can be as small as a microwave or as large as a trailer. The largest models can power vehicles, power plants, and even entire communities.

Enapter co-founder
Vaitea Cowan

HYDROGEN H2

Once isolated, hydrogen
can be stored for later use.

23

Catch and Clean
LanzaTech

Many are working hard to reduce fossil fuel use. The company LanzaTech is tackling the problem differently. It is catching, cleaning, and reusing greenhouse gases before they can cause harm.

LanzaTech captures pollution from power plants and factories before it leaves the smokestacks. The company then adds a specific kind of **bacteria** to the gases to change them into ethanol. This clean-burning fuel can power cars, buses, trucks, and even jets. Ethanol produces up to 97 percent fewer **emissions** than gasoline made from fossil fuels.

Captured gases can also be turned into plastic, rubber, or different kinds of textiles—materials typically made using fossil fuels. LanzaTech's recycled materials have been used in running shoes, athletic wear, and plastic containers.

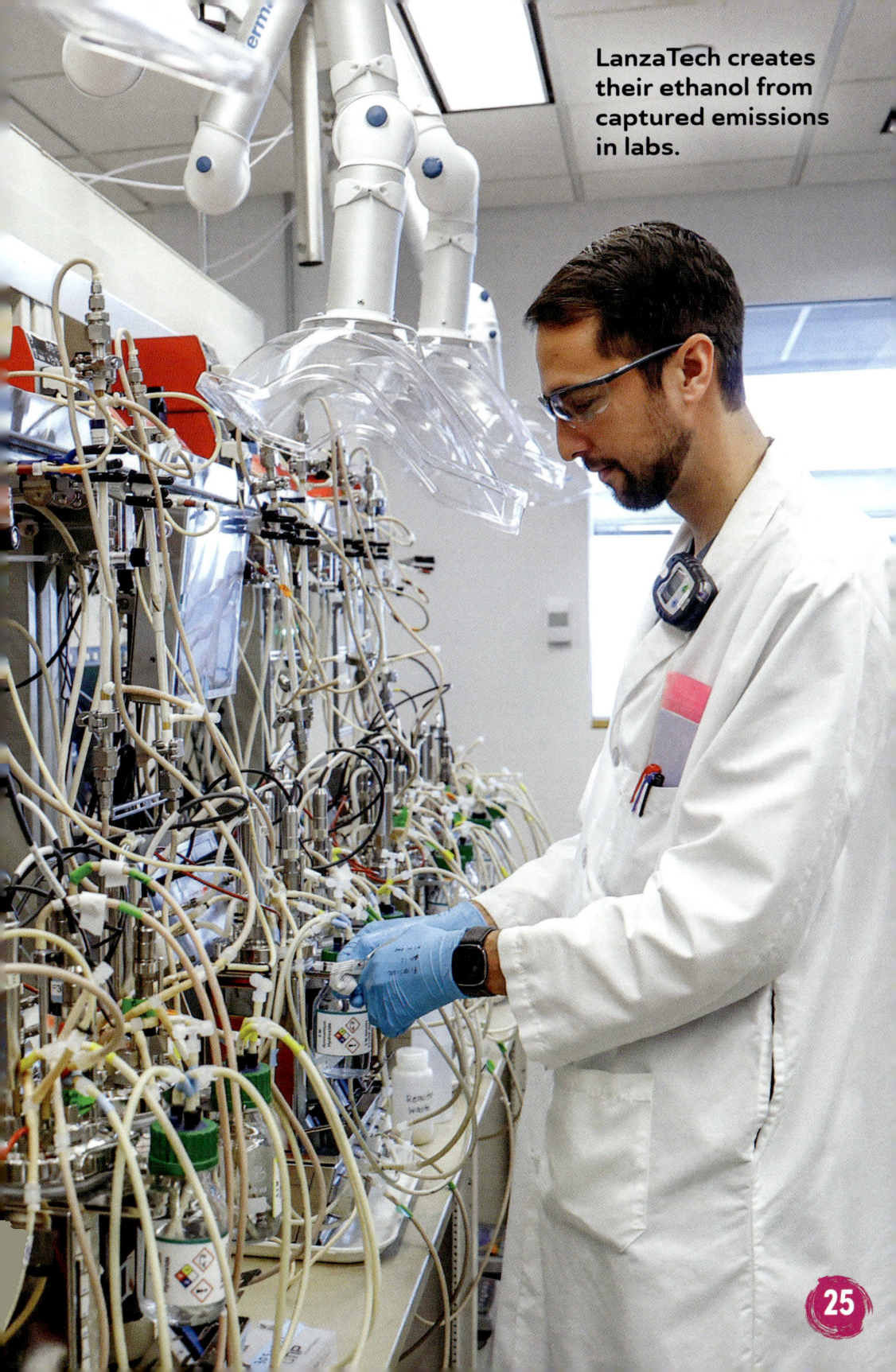

LanzaTech creates their ethanol from captured emissions in labs.

Renewing Our Future

Our future depends upon reducing our **reliance** on fossil fuels. Though the problem can seem overwhelming, there is reason to hope.

Every year, we power more and more of our world with green energy sources. As we make the shift, we put less strain on the planet. The clean and green future can be full of energy alternatives that are plentiful, renewable, and environmentally friendly. The solution is in the sunlight, wind, and water all around us!

Experiments are underway to tap into the power of ocean water. The motion of the waves and currents may be able to spin turbines to generate clean and renewable energy.

Go Green!

The best thing we can do to battle the harm caused as we power up is cut back on energy use. When we do need a charge, we can try to go green. Small steps can make a big impact.

Use solar-powered devices when possible. The sun can power calculators, watches, driveway lights, and much more.

Use LED lightbulbs, which use much less energy than fluorescent bulbs. Save even more electricity by turning off lights when you leave a room.

Unplug power cords and chargers when you're not using them. Turn off cell phones, computers, and game boxes when you're finished with them.

Heating water takes a lot of energy. Take short showers, and wash your clothes in cold water.

Instead of getting a car ride, walk or bike where you want to go whenever possible.

Glossary

atmosphere the layers of gases that surround Earth

bacteria tiny life-forms that can be seen only under a microscope

emissions substances, such as gases and soot, released into the air by fuel-burning engines

fossil fuels sources of energy made from the remains of animals and plants that lived long ago

geothermal having to do with heat from inside Earth

greenhouse gases gases that trap warm air in the atmosphere so it cannot escape into space

harnesses captures and puts to work

hydrogen a colorless, odorless gas found in the air

isolating breaking apart or away from other things

molecules small parts of matter that form when two or more atoms come together

oxygen a colorless gas found in air and water that people and other animals need to breathe

photovoltaic relating to the conversion of light energy into electricity

reliance dependence on something or need for support and assistance

renewable able to be replaced by natural processes

reservoirs natural or artificial holding areas for storing water

sediment tiny pieces of rock that break away from larger rocks

turbines machines that are turned by the wind, by flowing gases, or by moving water

Read More

Loureiro, Stephanie. *Fossil Fuels: A Graphic Guide (The Climate Crisis).* Minneapolis: Graphic Universe, 2023.

Thomas, Keltie. *Rising Seas: Flooding, Climate Change, and Our New World.* Buffalo, NY: Firefly Books, 2023.

Twamley, Erin, and Joshua Sneideman. *Renewable Energy: Power the World with Sustainable Fuel with Hands-On Science Activities for Kids.* Norwich, VT: Nomad Press, 2024.

Learn More Online

1. Go to **FactSurfer.com** or scan the QR code below.

2. Enter "**Using Green Energy**" into the search box.

3. Click on the cover of this book to see a list of websites.

Index

alternative 12, 26

atmosphere 10

burn 4, 6, 8, 10–12, 22, 24

coal 6, 8

devices 20, 22–23, 29

Dogger Bank Wind Farm 18–19

electricity 8, 12, 14, 16, 19–20, 29

Electrolyser 22–23

Enapter 22

factory 4, 24

fossil fuels 4, 6–12, 24, 26

gas 6–8

geothermal 16

Geysers 16

LanzaTech 24–25

Midong PV Farm 14–15

oil 6–8

Reeddi 20–21

renewable 12, 14, 16, 18, 26

solar 4, 14–15, 20, 29

steam 4, 12, 16

sunlight 4, 12, 14–15, 26

turbine 4, 12, 16, 18–19, 26

water 10, 12, 15–16, 22, 26, 29

wind 4, 12, 18–19, 26

About the Author

Raymond Bergin lives in New Jersey and Massachusetts. He makes the long drive between both places in a hybrid car that runs partly on electricity and uses much less gasoline. One day, he would love to drive a fully electric vehicle and install solar panels on his roof.